Chinese Proverbs:
Illustrated—annotated too!

Chinese

PROVERBS: extractions from
the book of historical fiction,
Stirring Li Chao

Proverbs:

Illustrated—annotated too!

S.E. Brandenburg

2017
Paha Sapa Press, S.D.

Chinese Proverbs: Illustrated; annotated too! is a work inspired by the book of historical fiction, <u>Stirring Li Chao</u> (published by Paha Sapa Press; 2016). Proverbs extracted from each of its thirty-three chapters forms the basis for written selections. Accompanying illustrations and annotations generally speak to the nature of the proverb and may or may not refer to any event described in <u>Stirring Li Chao</u>.

Paha Sapa Press, LLC
PO Box 621, Deadwood SD 57732

Printed in the United States of America
First edition, 2017

Publisher's Cataloging-in-Publication Data
provided by Five Rainbows Cataloging Services

Names: Brandenburg, S. E.
Title: Chinese proverbs : illustrated, annotated too! / S.E. Brandenburg.
Description: Lead, SD : Paha Sapa Press, 2017.
Identifiers: ISBN 978-0-9990885-9-3 (pbk.)
Subjects: LCSH: Proverbs, Chinese. | Proverbs, Oriental. | China--History--
    Taiping Rebellion, 1850-1864. | United States--Foreign relations--
    China. | China--Foreign relations--United States. | Illustrated books. |
    BISAC: LITERARY COLLECTIONS / Asian / Chinese. |
    REFERENCE / Quotations. | HISTORY / Asia / China.
Classification: LCC PN6519.C5 B73 2017 (print) | LCC PN6519.C5
    (ebook) | DDC 398.951--dc23.

Books may be purchased by contacting favorite booksellers, or by referring to the website, www.pahasapapress.com

Note to the Reader

Proverbs from this book parallel the chapters of Stirring Li Chao, the book inspired by actual events. In an attempt to strip situational truths to the bone (which is what proverbs do), strewn-out sentences or idle tidbits (like this) get eliminated. Proverbs, some say, are poetry. Some are borrowed from antithetical verses called "couplets." Devoted as the ancients were to finding the essence of things, they understood the virtue of simplicity. The verse, *"It's a gift to be simple"* is credited to the Shakers, but with such a profound appreciation for getting to the roots of things, understanding how purity and innocence emanate from the same loving source, the Chinese might have conceived it just as readily.

The mind shapes and polishes
a hundred thoughts that cluster round it

Proverbial wisdom predates history. Many proverbs (like wives' tales) have lost all formal connection with their human creators. Audibly, things passed down, and with the invention of writing a transcriber could place the pithy bits on scrolls. From there, translations and paraphrasing followed the linguistic styles most suited for the native tongue. What rolls off now ought approximate the original meaning.

The history behind *this* book is not so complicated. Chinese Proverbs allows its "parent" to breathe again, step back and let the simpler form take over, say what the elder had trouble communicating on its own. Curiosity brought *Stirring Li Chao* into existence. Query: **Why did Chinese wind up in the Wild West?**

Start off with something small and it snowballs. Intending to just scratch the surface, momentum carried me beyond that notion. What killed the cat plunged me into a bloody, 19th century civil/religious war ("un-American"—meaning that it was China's version, happening at relatively the same time). China's war bore a more pronounced Christian component. History courses I had taken never mentioned it, but the more I learned, the more my sensibilities became enraged—enough to birth (spew?) an entire book—Stirring Li Chao. For those interested in a more comprehensive understanding of the motives behind the occupation of China by nations of the West (as seen through the eyes of a young man from Manchuria), or wish to learn of America's role in helping to defeat *the only large-scale native Christian uprising the Chinese have ever experienced (upwards of thirty million died)*—please read on.

Knowing more about our contacts with China might bring some clarity to *why China is the way it is today*. For those who suspect there's something akin to karma working in the world today, *"rediscovering the past"* (the motto of Paha Sapa Press, publisher of these books) learning from the past makes sense. A seed of uncertain origin might have gotten in the mix of better minds to create a mindset of questionable merit. If such a pattern led America's leaders in the past, it's not unlikely that such influence continues to produce similar results today. More than one patriotic American has asked, **"Why do our leaders seem so intent on getting us into more wars?" We can't afford to police the world."** And underneath such questions are solemn acknowledgements: Arguably, regrettably, moronically, our policing makes more enemies than friends.

In the 19th century, the *official* policy of America was one of *"non-intervention."* Following the imperial footsteps of others, **America reversed its position and joined the military ranks of other westerners to defeat the popular Christian uprising** in China. As a result, *China was forced to buy and import opium from the occupying western forces.*

How's that for setting a good example? Christianity, anyone?

Again, for those who have *an inkling that something akin to karma might be at work, mysteriously acting behind the scenes* according to a universal principle resembling justice, some might observe the 21st century opioid maelstrom in the west. Sloughing off historical lessons and repeating the mistakes of the past is nonsensical. Believing that a book of proverbs will change anything is more than a leap of faith. To revisit the past requires an emptying of preconceived notions (an Eastern meditation approach—also too much for this small book). To revisit the past with fresh eyes might not be the same kind of "sudden illumination" sought in vipassana, but the insight might be "eye-opening" just the same.

What Paha Sapa Press hoped to present in its initial foray into "rediscovering history" was to offer an alternative to what might otherwise be an unwieldy, tedious study of American overseas military history. Stirring Li Chao, armed with historical facts and copious illustrations for proof, might give the everyday reader a sense of personal adventure while learning the truth behind today . . . the nature of things now—because today is a product of the past—following the universal law of cause and effect.

As a follow-up, while *Chinese Proverbs: Illustrated—annotated too!* borrows proverbs from the thirty-three chapters of its predecessor. The addition of over one-hundred illustration might be an early-childhood appreciation for "picture-books," but logically has just as much to do with recent studies of learning theory. For visual learners especially, these kinds of visual cues should aid overall retention and efficacy (after all, recalling a proverb at an opportune moment should be part of the fun). While some quotations have universal meaning, some are enigmatic enough to allow for a variety of interpretations—perfect soil for exploring ideas and exercising the power of critical thinking.

Annotations may provide additional insight. At the very least, this book of proverbs aims to give readers a better understanding of the historical interplay and interactions between countries and cultures. Confucius may have gotten credit for being the first to say, "all men are brothers," but sometimes the resemblance gets blurry. We don't look the same, don't act the same, don't sound the same. Nevertheless (which means just that—<u>never</u> less— there's always more to the story), as mortals in this or any other stretch of time, we all belong to one family. We're brothers and sisters . . . related to *a central, single source.*

CONTENTS

Observe the streams and springs to know the source of waters

(the Shijing *Book of Songs*; 600-800 BC)

A Traveler Contemplates a Waterfall. Zhang Lu. 1464-1528; PD-US

1

Without going out-of-doors,

one may know all under Heaven;

without peering through windows,

one may know the Way of Heaven

— Lao Zi

Better to light a candle

than curse the darkness.

S.E. Brandenburg

A hundred schools contend

Once upon a time ancient sages struggled with how to live, what to believe, how to conduct themselves and align with Heaven and Earth. Much discussion followed. After some time, many turned to the kings of old and the Daodejing (The Book of Changes). By living according to "the way," except for disciples of Zhuangzi who opposed Confucian order, Daoist sentiments could admit previous teachings of Confucius and allow for the introduction of Buddhist teachings too.

DAO,

the primordial vapor,

the source of all things;

a state of stillness when all things are

undifferentiated, a place called

"being embraced by the Dao."

A caged fowl has food,

but

the gravy pot is near

Author's Note:

(a scene from Chapter 1, <u>Stirring Li Chao</u>):

The pigeons clucked and stirred again.

"The pigeons are restless. Maybe they fear becoming Bing's next meal."

Smiling eyes turned toward the cages. The commotion continued.

"A caged fowl has food, but the gravy pot is near," *said Win Yu, citing an ancient adage.*

"Well, we can calm their anxious hearts by showing our best intentions." With a dash of muster, he said, "Let's eat rabbit instead. But, please forgive the small portions. I did not divine this pleasantry of having so many friends. This is good fortune of three lifetimes—more than double happiness!"*

~

* ui Bai (1050–1080), a prominent Chinese painter of the Northern Song Dynasty (960–1279), created the painting of *Magpies and Hare* (perhaps as a wedding gift). Mandarin pronunciation of *magpies* sounds like the word for *happiness*.

Therefore, seeing two magpies is symbolic of two happiness . . . or ***Double Happiness***.

"Magpies and Hare"

Cui Bai. *Magpies and Hare*. cc Wikimedia.org by Choufanging. PD-US

2

It takes more than one cold day
for a river to freeze three feet

It is not good to waste too many stones on one bird

Author's Note:

In the novel, an insensitive, unenlightened teacher uses this proverb to express the idea that trying to teach a dull student is a waste of resources.

S.E. Brandenburg

It's impossible to lift a dead dog over a wall

Author's Note:

Again, the teacher refers to a pupil he believes lacks the capacity to learn.

Wars are the parents
of hunger and misery

Dying Lion of Lucerne, a monument and landmark in Switzerland

S.E. Brandenburg

The same sun that turns a grass green, turns a grass brown

Let the river flow around the rigid pillars of Confucius

Ancient Gate Ruins, the Pillars Old Summer Palace
(*Yuanming Yuan*) Beijing, China, destroyed by British and French Army in 1860 Second Opium War

Author's Note:

At the time, who could predict how successive generations would feel about the wisdom of Confucius? Regardless, none would have been able to envision the pillaging of the priceless artwork by the West—or the destruction of the pillars holding up the Old Summer Palace.

S.E. Brandenburg

3

When men discuss the things to come, the rats laugh in the rafters

Author's Note:

Li Chao has a plan—which leads him to "The Teahouse." Hoping to learn the whereabouts of "Old Illustrious" from an informal gaggle of regulars, due to a healthy (slanderous?) repartee, Chapter 3 is chock full of proverbs. The clamor inside revolves around the discussion of man's "better half." (The lack of Illustrations allows readers absolute control over their own free-ranging imaginations.)

It might be well to note that prior to the establishment of patriarchy, *in Daoist lore, the female essence played an indispensible role in creation* (symbolized by the Mysterious Female and Mother Earth). And, after the discovery and realization that the pristine nature of humans and harmony with nature had been lost, antiquities speak of a *female leader who "patched the sky with five-colored stones."* (It might also be noted that in traditional Chinese symbolism, the sky represents the mind . . . hmmm.)

~

(The Scene: *inside the teahouse. Men in active discussion concerning females*)

"Woman is a child," said a man about his concubine.

"What else?" said another.

"Woman is a perfect spectacle of fury!"

"Every mouse becomes an elephant!"

"Like the reflection of moon in water, the same distance separates a wife from reason," said the next man in succession.

"Be wary of a tempestuous woman. You may get your neck wrung like a chicken," said a cracked voice with a ludicrous face, applying a stranglehold hand to his throat.

"A genuine cat slays a mouse. A genuine man rules the house," declared a thumping fist on the table.

"It's best to leave a dragon in its lair. Do this—or get ready to kneel for punishment."

"The prudent man must pay a price for peace."

"What's the price for a clamorous wife?"

"Even a grunting pig gets exhausted with constant uproars."

"Keep your noisy wife indoors! *One dog can set the whole village to howling!*" said a slim man with a sly wide grin, waving his hands in all directions.

A quieter man spoke to say, "Some women *do* know how to bridle a tongue."

A widower intervened, trying to keep the table turning the same direction with another stroke of concord. *"Even on the chin of a dragon, one must endeavor to grope for a pearl."*

One man's face had fallen. He wore a look of dejected gloom as he muttered a quiet, *"It's not possible to gather spilt water."*

A moment of reflection followed. *"Girls live as frogs in a well."*

"This is why *the female child wishes to be born again as a dog—so she can have the freedom to wander.*"

The mood had become somber. An eye turns to Li Chao, sensing that a new perspective might help. When asked to comment on what he's been hearing, surprisingly, his answer is quick.

"Bleating sheep lose many mouthfuls."

The men became bemused again. They asked more questions of Li Chao. One answer ended the volley. Faces grew concerned. Talking stopped. Pipes puffed. Thoughts rolled around in the smoke before anyone spoke. It was a puzzle.

Out of a thousand answers, one is wisest," said a man with the largest belly, "but even a superior being doesn't advise another on which trail to travel. Each person has a different destiny."

A peasant must stand for a long time on a hillside with his mouth open before a roast duck flies in

Author's Note:

Though looking nothing like the illustration, in the book, Li Chao became awestruck. His jaw dropped. Silence, incense, and prayers for Li Chao's benefit enveloped the room. Such concern from men he barely knew was far beyond what Li Chao could have imagined. The aptly spoken, a proverb mirrored the expression of grateful surprise on Li Chao's face.

S.E. Brandenburg

4

Great doubts, big wisdom

5

One must start with the right premise

or miss the truth by a thousand suns

People sleep best just before dawn;

just before death, people get wise

Portrait of an Old Man in an Armchair. Rembrandt (1654)Wikimedia commons PD-US

Pluck the ripe plum before it wrinkles

Author's Note:

Li Chao consulted the oracle, Yi Jing (I Ching). Old Illustrious interpreted and said, *"When the opportunity presents itself and times are favorable, leap! And don't forget the potential of opposites!"*

6

A brother will cross a sea of a thousand miles to redeem the honor of a bankrupt brother

From the loving example of one family, a whole State may become loving

— Confucius

S.E. Brandenburg

7

It is easy to dodge a spear that comes in front of you, but hard to avoid an arrow shot from behind

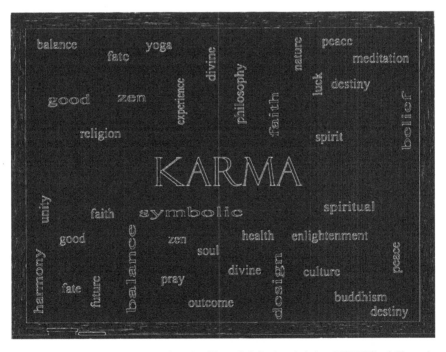

8

He who deliberates fully before taking a step will spend his entire life on one leg

A pebble of truth is does not make a river crossing

S.E. Brandenburg

The lotus root may be severed, but its threads are still connected

A man should not travel to a distant place while his parents are still alive

S.E. Brandenburg

A good son
does not climb high

David Wood, the cliff footpath CCby SA3.o Wikimediacommons

"Footpath on the Edge of the Cliff"
(Tian Menshan Mountain National Park, Zhangjiajie, NW Hunan Province)

Author's Note:

Ninety-nine bends in the road parallel the edge-of-the-cliff footpath. Some sections, constructed of glass, to see the sight and sense the fright, allow the walker to view the distance of a potential fall. Many choose the cable car or minibus to reach the beginning of the ninety-nine steps leading up to . . .

"Heaven's Gate"

Tian Menshan Mountain National Park, Zhangjiajie, NW Hunan Province Huangdan2060 (2010)
Wikimedia.org

S.E. Brandenburg

9

When a son goes a three thousand li,

a mother grieves.

The fly that plays too long in the candle singes his wings at last

S.E. Brandenburg

If you live near the mountain, you will live by it; if you live near the water, you will live by it

The sky is big
and the emperor
is far away

S.E. Brandenburg

The difference between yes and certainty, how meaningless—but the difference between good and evil— how immeasurably great   – Laozi

"Archangel Michael Fighting with Dragon"
engraving of Nazareene School, published in The Holy Bible, St. Vojtech Publishing, Trnava, Slovakia, 1937
Copyright: <a href='https://www.123rf.com/profile_miriamataneckova'>miriamataneckova >

S.E. Brandenburg

12

Often one finds destiny
where one hides to avoid it

Hidden Dragon

Author's note:

Hidden dragons and crouching tigers may also refer to undiscovered persons of exceptional ability.

S.E. Brandenburg

13

When a person walks, he leaves traces. When a bird flies, it leaves feathers

14

For inner self to advance, the sage withdraws; lose self to preserve self

— Laozi

Author's note:

"Losing self" can be a simple matter, i.e.
*Watching someone fishing, one is lost
in a world of water and mist.*

Live among quiet rivers.
Harmonize thoughts

S.E. Brandenburg

The knock of night does not bother a clear conscience

15

The frost and moon exchanging brightness

One good thing leads to another

S.E. Brandenburg

Distant water can't quench
an immediate thirst

Author's Note:

Sometimes refreshment is nearer than a shadow. *Amid the parched and spoiled Shanghai streets, water refreshed its newest residents.* Most commonly, the word "refreshment" is associated with the sensation of drinking, a satisfaction related to a physical thirst, but for a soul dried up from living too long in a spiritual desert, the *replenishing* is the gift of life.

16

The water being clear, count the stones and fish

17

Riding backwards on a cow, the herd-boy returns from yonder worlds

Respect out of fear, never genuine;

reverence out of respect, never false

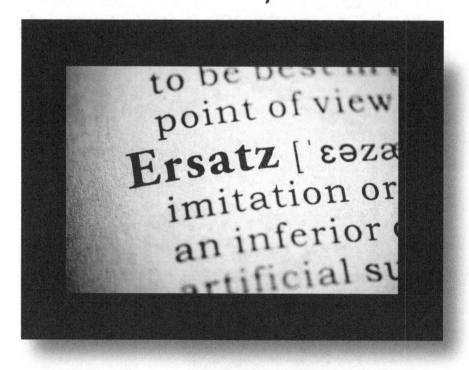

Author's note:

Counterfeits are knock-offs. Fawning out of fear or to wheedle favor causes the lie-bearer to try to "pass fish eyes off for pearls." Respect for someone truly worthy is a glorious thing.

18

Bad things never walk alone

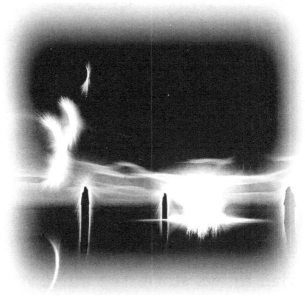

Author's Note:

Myriad things storm the mind. **Anger directed toward the obvious may miss an even greater threat.** The real adversary is subtle, appearing not as an enemy, but as a comrade fighting a common battle. The decoy is the madman out in front. Meanwhile, the Trojan horse is accepted and gets inside. Distraction is an ancient technique of war. While the focus is on the grandstand, the *subtler* "bad things" walk right in—wherein lies the power to produce far more distressing outcomes.

S. E. Brandenburg

Puck

THE OLD STORY.

Published in 1900, the cover issue of this periodical illustrates an international situation at the time. Entitled, **"The Old Story,"** the cat wears clerical robes. It bears the label, "missionary." It toys and paws at the roasting chestnut (China). The monkey, representing the European powers, gloats with superiority.

Just as "bad things never walk alone," if genuine investigative journalists still have a voice and platform, and political cartoonists have no poloitical agenda but to work for "everyman's" rights and equal treatment, gross injustices will not appear as isolated occurrences either. Good things can congregate too.

Under the same distaste for its government's role in international affairs as the British, *Puck*, a French cartoon of the same era shows the situation even more graphically. "China" leans back in a barber's chair. "France" stands overhead. A funnel is placed in the Chinaman's mouth. The French pour a bucket of opium down China's throat. Figuratively, and literally, opium got forced down China's throat!

(If sure this cartoon resided in the public domain, I'd publish it. If you're familiar with it, please inform?)

Once bitten by a snake, even a rope may frighten you

If you have only two coins, buy a loaf of bread with one, and a lily with the other

Author's note:

The fragrance is universal. It seems the country of origin of this proverb is uncertain.

S.E. Brandenburg

If a nation's treasures are stolen,

its reserves reside in its scholars

Statue of Confucius; Wikimedia commons

Author's Note:

Confucius, born in the 6th century BC, China, is so closely associated with the word, "scholar" as to nearly make them synonymous. Various temples and abundant artwork throughout the ages stand as a testimony to the lasting reverence for Confucius.

Confucius and His Students: Ming Dynasty; Wikimedia Commons

Confucius and His Students: Ming Dynasty; Wikimedia Commons

S.E. Brandenburg

Scholars, civil servants appointed by the emperor (also known as *literati*), along with the *scholar gentry* who'd earned academic degrees by passing imperial examinations, dominated the government until the middle of the 19th century. ***Concerned with what was perceived to be deterioration in general morals among the populace and corruption within the government,*** scholars in the late Northern Song Dynasty *looked to the arts to reestablish or cultivate ethical behavi*or. **Believing the** *past to be morally superior* **to the present**, scholars encouraged the reawakening of painting and calligraphy. In addition to a scholarly pursuit of the arts, the scholar gentry had other responsibilities. As officials within villages, they also taught in schools, helped to resolve minor legal disputes, assist in collecting taxes and disseminate teachings of Confucius—all the while exemplifying the precepts and virtues contained in Confucian moral teachings.

PHILOSOPHORUM SINENSIUM

PRINCIPIS
CONFUCII
VITA

UM FU CII, *sive* Confucius, quem Sinenses uti Principem Philosophiae suae sequuntur, & colunt, vulcari vel domestico patrio nomine Kiu a dictis, cognomento Chum-ni, natalem habent sedem in Regno Lu, (quod Regnum hodie Xantum annexum Imperii Ciu, ye territorij Chum pim, quod ad orientalem Kio son pertinet; hac autem tractu paret sibi Yen-chou dicta. Natus est anno ... Imperii ... in Lum-vam sunt hic tertiæ & trigesimo è tertia Familia, seu ... Imperatoria, Cheu dicta, quit is annus 47. Kem sio dicte ... tricesimo & tricesimo avum Siam ... in Regis, que ea tempestate Regnum Lu obtinebat; die 11. undecimæ lunæ Kem-yo dicte, sub & tum vestis jemestres, que ante (hujus totum ... Matter ei fuit Chun, è familia pram bili Yen venusta; Pater No leam he, qui non solum prisci ordinis Magistratus, quem gessit in Regno Sam, sed generis qui quo nobilitate suit illustris; stirpem quippe duxit suam Chronica Sinensium testantur, & tabulis genealogica, que annalibus inferuntur, perspicuæ docet) ex an. sive genitura Imperator Ti ye è a. familia Xam. Porro natus est Confucius Patre jam septuagenario, quam ades tricenta in suis mos ausit; sed Matre populis deinde suscepta; suit per annos unum & vigenti, congive in monte Tum tam Regni Lu pejiclo. Puer jam jescunas prematura quadam maturitate, neve, quam pueris similive, cum a quasibus negquam vesci & luptare, Oblata edulia non ante delibabat, quam prisa tita, que sua ceu annutaretur, cælo recusabundus delibabit. Adumorum quindecim adolescens totum se dedere cæpit priscorum libris evolvendis, & rejectis iis, que minus utilia videbantur, optima quaque

Cg

Life and Works of Confucius; Prospero Intorcetta, Philippe Couplet *et al.* (1687

Around the fourth century B.C., society got divided into four classes: *the scholar elite, landowners and farmers, the craftsman,* and lastly, *the merchants.* On the top on the totem pole, the scholar elite, to emulate the ways of Confucius, advocated for the simple rural life (a lifestyle thought to best facilitate a moral education).

"Scholar in a Meadow" 11th century/Anonymous)

柳陰高士李晉爲
高枝浪耶軟意
自家祝閩伊人
阿咥氏长唐房
李晉勿詢
丁亥长月沙瓷

Chinese Proverbs: Illustrated—annotated too!

Farmers and craftsmen produced useful things, items necessary for society. For their contribution they earned a degree of respect. The merchants, on the other hand, selling for profit, developed and encouraged a taste for luxury (among other things). Within the realm of Confucian ethics, they added nothing of value to a moral society. Consequently, the merchants occupied the lowest rung of the social ladder.

The concern the ancients had about deteriorating morals among the populace and corruption within the government is not limited to China—or a time period. Older generations tend to believe the younger generation, comparatively speaking, lack morals, and a universal opinion might suggest that the "good-old-days" were superior to the present. What stands out here, however, is not just the awareness of a problem, but the solutions chosen to reestablish ethics. Turning to the arts, they also give a thumbs-up for the simple life.

S.E. Brandenburg

"The Open Court" (1887); Carus, Paul, (1852-1919)

"The Open Court" illustrates the many-faceted nature of influential figures leading up to China's entrance into the 20th century. The dragon, the symbol of Heaven, takes center stage. On its back is a tortoise shell, anciently ascribed to the invention of writing (mysterious too, for its link to the Yijing). Many notable scholars appeared throughout China's long history, but the *Three Noble Teachers* remain the most influential.

"Confucius presenting the young Guatama Buddha to Laotzi"

Ming Dynasty;Wikimedia;CC-PD

S.E. Brandenburg

Author's Note:

Scholar-officials became associated with the *Four Accomplishments*: painting, poetry, a strategic board game (similar to chess), and playing the zither. Beginning in the Yuan dynasty, scholars developed an expressive style of paintings that sought to recreate the inner spirit of landscapes, as well as the inner spirit of the painter.

Clearly, despite the many responsibilities assigned to their position, the literati enjoyed a life of leisure. Confucius couldn't have foreseen how militant nations in the west would eventually loot and burn both the summer and winter palaces. Debates surrounding the role and efficacy of the literati during the time of Western occupation, coupled with the defeat of the Christian enthusiasts (the Taiping) leave some to speculate on differing outcomes. The world is nearly unanimous in assuming that a nation's treasures, as well as its reserves, lay within the physical realm, but, in the long run, what *really* constitutes a nation's reserves? Its treasures?

The following characters bear some resemblance to each other. Perhaps these ancient symbols provide clues as to how the ancients perceived a commonality between certain traits and associated virtues. With only a superficial knowledge of the language, as to how these characters originated in the minds of their creators remains a mystery, but to an outsider, it seems that the words "Knowledge" and "Harmony" share a close alignment.

KNOWLEDGE

HARMONY

Though a faint resemblance still appears, these look less like . . .

WEALTH

19

A mantis stalking a cicada is unaware of an oriole behind

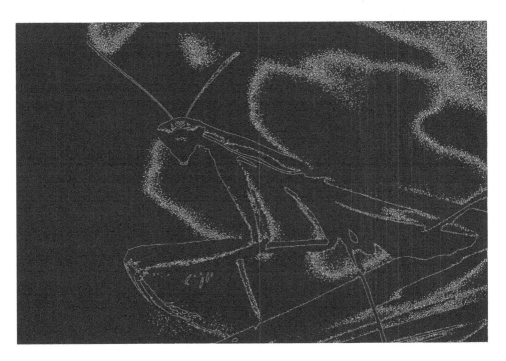

Author's note:

Maybe not bigger than a leaf, but if I were the cicada,
I'd hope the oriole hurries.

S.E. Brandenburg

More pleasant than a planned meeting, is one by accident

Flies do not visit an egg with no crack

This stone from Mount Tai
dares to oppose

Author's Note:

According to many, four classical novels of Chinese Literature stand out as exceptional: *Water Margin (Outlaws of the Marsh), Romance of the Three Kingdoms, Journey to the West,* and *Dream of the Red Chamber (the Story of the Stone).* The inscription on the stone (see illustration) first appears in the Dream of the Red Chamber. In its original conception, the stone is sentient. The stone also found a role to play in the book, Stirring Li Chao.

> *Truth becomes fiction when fiction's true*
> *Real becomes not-real when the unreal's real.*

— from the opening chapter of <u>Dream of the Red Chamber</u>

Written between the 14th and 18th centuries, these historical novels are among the oldest and *longest in the world*. The extended prose narrative appealed to the increasingly literate population.

(A scene from "Chronicles of the Stone". Public domain artwork by Xu Bao. PD-US

S.E. Brandenburg

To know the road ahead, ask those coming back

Author's note:

This is another of those sound-like Chinese proverbs that may not have originated in China.

20

Distant water won't put out

a fire close at hand

Author's Note:

True enough, but not all fires need extinguishing. Would a burning bush, all by itself, capture your attention? What if it talked?

What is heaven's reason?

Yin/Yang; Bagua (Eight Trigrams)
(carved into a temple rock, north china)

Author's Note:

The Bagua is central to Daoist cosmology. Divination, the art of reading the patterns of the universe to intuit the flux, permanence, and interdependence of all things, and *feng-shui* (pronounced "fung shway") rely on the eight interrelated fundamental principles of reality.

21

He who travels a lot becomes wise;
he who is wise stays home

The *"Wisdom Path"* leading to the Heart Sutra,
Lantau Island, Hong Kong

Author's Note:

B uddist stone carvings on Mount Taishan in the Shandong province of China inspired a professor to create the Heart Sutra text on Lantau

Island, Hong Kong. A figure-eight configuration (symbolic of infinity) of thirty-eight timbers received the calligraphy carvings in 2005. A timber at the highest point on the hill remains blank. This suggests "emptiness" (a key theme in the Heart Sutra and Mahayana sutra).

Everything arises from conditions . . . "if". Li Chao listens to Old Illustrious repeat this well-known truth—and the simplicity makes him anxious to learn what he doesn't already know. But, some truths deserve repeating. *Everything* arises from conditions . . . *if*—conditions are adequate. *Everything* is in a constant process of change, and by understanding the relativity of things, by making good use of available conditions a freedom arises for the attainment of perfect harmony and bliss. Whether moody or blue, a proverb from China or sung in the west, travel can be beneficial . . . and *thinking is a good way to travel.*

A fall into a ditch makes you wiser

Author's Note:
(pertaining to *a scene in Chapter 21*)

On the long journey to Canton, Li Chao experiences a number of falls—but why the fall on purpose?

22

Water thrown out is hard to put back in the container

No sweet berry can live in desert

S.E. Brandenburg

23

A book holds a house of gold

A sinking boat cannot be mended in the middle of a river

S.E. Brandenburg

Take a feather from every goose—but not just one— always.

Weasel comes to say "Happy New Year!" to the chickens

Animal preaching to Chicken

anonymous; 1440-1450 The Morgan org. PD-US

Author's note:

The passage of centuries doesn't dull the warning.

S.E. Brandenburg

The Dao that can be named

is not the Dao.

— Laozi

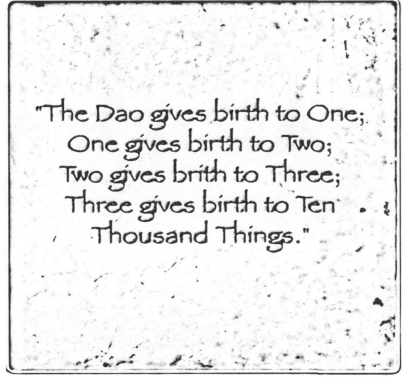

(excerpt from the Daodejing)

Words that are argumentative do not reach the point

— *Zhuangzi*

Zhuangzi Dreaming of a Butterfly. Ike no Taiga (Japan 1723-1776) PD-US

Author's note:

Zhuangzi (AKA: Zhuang Zhou/Chuang Tzu), an influential Daoist philosopher of the 4th century B.C. wrote of many things. A surprising amount survives up to the present day.

Old body carries energy
to other places

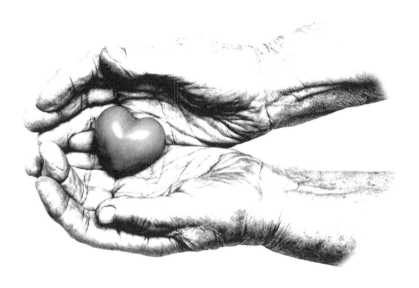

Chinese Proverbs: Illustrated—annotated too!

A book is like a garden
to carry in pocket

Author's note:

Again, sounding more Oriental than Occidental, the origin of this is also disputed. In the book, a pastor-friend of Li Chao turns this proverb into a dirty? joke (not really).

S.E. Brandenburg

24

When good luck comes, even the wind expedites the journey

Author's note:

Chinese junk in the foreground and a Western steamship in background. The wind cannot be seen with the eye, but we can observe the effects of it.

Enough shovels of earth someday makes a mountain

Author's Note:

"Yin Yang and the Art of Digging?"

In this scenario, the valley and mountain would arrive together, simultaneously co-created, synchronous and in harmony.

Hidden dragons, crouching tigers

卧 wò
crouching

虎 hǔ
tiger

藏 cáng
hiding

龍 lóng
dragon

26

Concealing truth is to wear embroidered clothes and travel by night

TRUTH

Author's Note:

The notion of truth and a cover-up is complex. Wisdom weighs the cost of limelight. Flaunting wealth is one thing. Concealing it is another. Bearing a tangential resemblance, Zhuangzi said, *"To be poured* <u>*into*</u> *without becoming full, and pour* <u>*out*</u> *without becoming empty . . . without knowing how this is brought about . . . this is the art of* **'concealing the light**

When word and action are pure, happiness follows like an unshakable shadow

>

S.E. Brandenburg

27

Talk doesn't cook rice

28

Pure gold does not fear the furnace

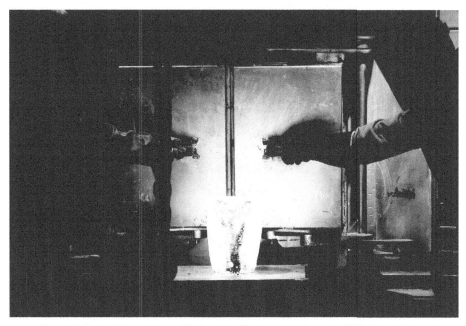

Better a good deed at home than burning incense far away

FAMILY

S.E. Brandenburg

Author's Note:

The Chinese, over many thousands of years, adopted a code of "Traditional Virtues." Among these are *Benevolence, Righteousness, Propriety, Wisdom* and *Fidelity*. Arising from Confucianism, these comprise the **Five Constant Virtues**.

Of the **"Five Relationships,"** most revolve around family. Even when old enough to leave and establish a separate residence, traditionally, and by choice, the Chinese tend to stick close to home. Often, if at all possible, they share the same roof with other generations. If this cannot be accommodated, most return home as frequently as conditions allow.

Thus, the saying, *"falling leaves returning to the root of the tree that sired them."*

29

Those who seek revenge must remember to dig two graves

30

A mountain of knives and a sea of fire

31

A person cannot be judged by his appearance anymore than a sea can be measured with a bucket

Author's note:

It would be like trying to ...

Measure the sea with an oyster shell

32

Do not anxiously hope for that which is not yet come; do not vainly regret what is already past

Seek fish on a tree?

Author's note:

Though the proverb alludes to inadequate methods, from high above, Li Chao finds the only fish in the world that will do—the perfect fish.

S.E. Brandenburg

Men in the game are blind to what observers see clearly

Author's note:

She's hard to spot, but with outreaching eyes and gentle persuasion, the "Mother of the World" applies a guiding hand. East or West, the best of mothers coax the best of rhythms.

"Mothers hold their hands for a short while, but their hearts forever."

33

All the past died yesterday;

the future is born today

"Temperance"; fresco, Ambrogio Lorenzetti (1285-1348) PD-US

Author's Note:

Temperance would smile upon the inscriptions at Delphi—
"*Know thyself*" and "*Nothing in excess*"—but in seeing how
the sands of time run out on man, and how the hourglass
sits aright both ways, might she deem it prudent to invert
the bulbs—and let them have a go at it again?

There's a circular slab, a sundial in modern day Beijing.
Speared straight through, pointing to both earth and sky, to
past and future does it seem, (the present somewhere
between). Year after year, shadows track the daily hours, but
of the sunken stem, what Arthurian pull liberates all of
time?

S.E. Brandenburg

The subtlest of all subtleties, this is the gateway to all mysteries

— Laozi

(The Book of Changes / I Ching / Daodejing)

Author's Note:

As in life, _Stirring Li Chao_ comes to an end—really?

The door gaped open. A walk in the clouds would mean an instant end of earthen days, but in the twinkling of an eye, the same door shown a simple prison cell. If imprisoned like a book-stuck flower, he'd do just that, mark his time like Bunyon did and write—and for a tortured spell Li Chao tried, but with the knot of love still twisted, all he'd scrawled were but idle crawlings on the wall. Something had died. Yet, something remained alive.

Epilogue

(copied from the book, <u>Stirring Li Chao</u>)

John Bunyon, the author of <u>The Pilgrim's Progress: From This World To That Which Is to Come</u>, as a preface to his work, penned what he called, "The Author's Apology For His Book."

By happenstance, I read this odd prelude only after finishing the final chapter of <u>Stirring Li Chao</u>. It seemed more than incidental. This curiosity expressed what I had just gone through. In some sense, what I'd scarcely completed seemed to be a prequel to what I'd originally started out to do. Without belaboring this fascination, I'll quote the opening lines of Bunyon's "Apology":

> *"When at the first I took my pen in hand*
> *Thus for to write, I did not understand*
> *That I at all should make a little book*
> *In such a mode; nay, I had undertook*
> *To make another; which when almost done,*
> *Before I was aware, I this begun."*

Bunyon's pilgrim sought to pass through the "wicket gate" to reach the Celestial City. Li Chao, on the other hand, God willing, if he should happen to find a gateway and resume his journey to the West, might divine that he's headed for a city more infernal than sublime.

— S.E. Brandenburg

destiny's knot

Chinese Proverbs: Illustrated; annotated too!

Made in the USA
Las Vegas, NV
12 April 2025

20853555R00085